Times, Tides & Seasons

Steve Smith

First Printing: 2026
Estuary Publishing
ISBN: 978-1-0369-6228-9

Contents

About The Author

Steve Smith is now retired after working in the world of Autism and Asperger Syndrome for 30 years and has lived in South Wales for the last twenty years with his wife Issie. They have two married children and three grandchildren.

He previously published a slim volume of poetry called *Edge of Silence.*

Steve loves, music, spirituality, reading, jogging, football and spending time with his family.

He began writing as a teenager and returned to it after a long break, and his desire in writing is to write from the heart to touch the hearts of others.

"The poet with a depth of heart, evokes love and beauty with words"

Melanie Anne Kettner-Borough

"Love your heart, you have managed to put into words what I find hard to express and my heart resonates with"

The late Helen Brewster

"Love your poems. They give me a thirst for deep encounters in sacred silence"

Jan Mayers

"This is so profound and powerful. Thank you for sharing your amazing gift. It touches hearts and transforms people"

Trudie De Graf

"A nice blend of darkness and light. I like your poetry. It cuts to the chase and has some profound and yet simple and accessible imagery"

Tony Clay, musician and songwriter

"When you write you are drawing from a deep well and you can see that others recognise this too by their responses to these poems"

Tim O'Hare, musician and songwriter

"Steve lives out of a deep revelation of the peace of God and brings that to those who have the privilege of knowing him. His poems are gifts to take us on a journey deeper into the Father's heart"

Karen Lowe, Co-Founder of Antioch Church Llanelli

"I meditate on your poetry with beautiful pictures of waterfalls and rivers, and it was a very good moment with our Father, Jesus and the Holy Spirit"

Guy Zeller.

These are a collection of poems that I've written over the last few years in different parts of the world which have often been a real inspiration for writing. Living just five minutes away from the Wetlands in South Wales and the coastal estuary I've seen the geese and many other birds flying in and then leaving from many different nations and "Like migrating geese we also followed the winds, crossed the seas, and watched the tides"

Here I am now so aware of the changing seasons, the subtle light that alters daily, the dance of nature, and the rhythm of the changing months.

The wheel of the world is still turning ever onwards.

A New Year

The wheel of the year turns onwards. Standing at the gates and hearing a new song rising. Walking into the unknown country of a New Year. We've never been this way before.

Into the Wild

Spread your wings and fly
On the winds of the dawn
Knowing the call of the wild
comes calling again.
Into that unknown country
Crossing new frontiers
to what is beyond.
See snowcapped mountain peaks
and golden eagles soar
and where we meet
the tenderness of wolves and bears
Heart of an explorer.
I hear this song
at the turning of the year
calling me again
into the wild.

Like The Flight of the Falcon

Like the flight of the falcon
Soaring on the wings of the wind
Like the breath-taking hawk
or dazzling wild geese turning south
high in the pale ice blue sky,
so other pilgrim travellers
cross the mountains to what is beyond.
Heart of explorers, explorers of heart
Travelling light to the Gate of Awakening.
And now a new road opens,
Beckons us, calls us again
And so, the heart our last frontier.
It's always been a journey,
but now it's the journey within.
There always was a journey
And now it's a journey of heart.
Open roads, open skies, open heart.
Come healing winds come blow
upon the journey of my heart.

Sometimes winter drags on and on with no end in sight. Will spring ever come? And then one day, early on, something starts to change.

Cold Days of Winter

It's been a long cold winter
and some of us now watching for signs
in these slow-moving minutes and days.
Still cocooned, weaving our dreams.
on the loom of our hearts.
Looking for early stirrings
of earth, leaf, shoots and sap
that come like the poetry
of our own unfolding.
Then days come when tectonic plates shift
shaking the ground beneath our feet.
The dark will bloom and sing again
in this wild silence when
hope lights up these
hard winter skies.

The Old Harbour. A favourite place to come. There was a time I came here every week to find the silent space between the breathing in and breathing out, and the place of stillness. To come and hear the song of the sea, and see the skies open even on the stormiest of days. This was written in memory of Kay whose words inspired some of this poem.

Fragrant Pines in Winter

An Ice-cold morning, and walking
through frost on fragrant pines
to this place of open skies
where oyster catchers gather and heron
stretches its wings to glide across the old harbour.
This place
where light echoes and reflects
deep waters and roar of tides.
This place
of stones of terracotta, blue, grey,
and copper red.
Sometimes depending on the wind
you can hear the church bells
across the fields.
This place.
A haven, a harbour, a home
to where I come to find
the silent space between
the breathing in....and breathing out.
And here an ocean of possibilities.
Watching the winds change
and thankful for this extra light.

February is traditionally known as a month of transition, as spring begins to beckon. We're already watching the gradual lengthening of the days and very small glimpses of fresh colour as the year continues to unfold.

The Great Unfolding

At last, the days of February come
To greet us as old friends
Then days come when tectonic plates shift
shaking the ground beneath our feet.
The dark will bloom and sing again
in this wild silence when
hope lights up these
hard winter skies.

Spring

"Even in these darkest days, and places,
yet still you come Oh Spring"

Welcome the first days of the new season, season of hope. It's a new day, new seeds of hope. Let hope rise afresh in your heart, and hope means hearing the new melody of the future and daring to dream again. For ten years we lived in a house where I was amazed to see the yearly explosion of golden colours out of an apparent dead bush in the garden.

Spring

It's been a long cold winter
bitter winds blown across the estuary.
Looking from my window I've watched that bush
that shrivelled dead bleak barren bush
battered by cold winter winds.
March comes and brings early promise.
Flecks of gold on branch appears.
Hints of hope spring up become vibrant lemon
yellow.
Forsythia sings spring!
This morning from my window
sunshine streams down
upon that bush.
Blaze afire with life
luminous fire-bright bush.
Transfigured.
Keeps burning.

Many of us are living in the tension between knowing the hope of seeing the season of spring yet also seeing the horrors of war on the daily news. Yet spring still comes and even in the darkest of days seeds begin to grow, and trees blossom again.

First Light of Spring

Even in these darkest days
yet still you come, Oh spring!
This the great up-rising, rebellion
Against death, decay and war.
Now new stirrings, awakenings
Of earth, sky, trees and plant.
Spring? You always come again.
These seeds of hope now grow, burst forth
in colours of the dawn.
In desert places too spring comes
where stunning crocus bloom,
Even desert places of our hearts
are touched again by light as
This earth's axis tilts towards the sun.
Spring? We welcome you
even in these darkest times.

I wrote this in the early part of the Covid pandemic lockdown in March 2020.We really didn't know what was going to happen next, but certainly the door to travelling slammed shut. There were pictures of city centres eerily deserted, and appalling pictures of devastation across the world.
Eventually life began to gradually return to normal, but it didn't happen quickly. Those of us that lived through these days will not forget.

In The Year of the Plague

When the shadow moved across our land.
When the plague dogs howled at midnight.
When the winds of death blew through the streets.
We remember.
When the raven stalked the evening skies.
When the tears they fell at midnight.
When the sound of grief was heard on high.
We remember.
When the shadow lifted from our land.
When we woke to skies so clear,
Wildflowers and the singing of the birds.
Stepping out, dazzled, dream again,
Into a world where everything had changed.
New song rising but we will never forget.
    We will never forget,
        These plague days.

Shadows fell on our world with the invasion of Ukraine by Russia. Such tragedies, pain, death and chaos of a beautiful land that we had visited in 2018. In Spring 2022 we were seeing terrible images of the suffering of people in the siege of Mariupol every night on the news.

Lament For Mariupol

Oh, Mariupol city of death and tears
may your name be forever
burnt upon our hearts and minds
for a thousand generations.
They sat amongst the smoke and ash
Saying " when the well ran out
we had to melt snow on an open fire
as shells fell all around like rain. And
when we had no snow there was no water,
not even for the little ones"

Who will be a witness of these evil days?
Oh, Mariupol how long?
May your name be forever
scorched into our souls
even for a thousand generations.
Just a solitary nightingale,
singing through the dark,
waiting for the dawn
    We will not forget.

I visited the island of Bardsey of the coast of North Wales for a week's retreat in early spring. No gas, no electricity, no running water and just a small boat to cross the currents! I climb high on the rocks and sit watching the movement of the tides, tasting the salt in the breeze, and breathe again.... ....

Island of Moving Tides

There is an ocean of colour
before me.
From turquoise blue, deep greens
and mercury grey
Shafts of silver through dark clouds
and dazzling white light
illuminates. Sun sparkles.

A tapestry, a patchwork
ever changing, moving sea
spreads before me.
Below hard rock, grasses
and seabirds cry.

There are moments when
You open innocent eyes.
New ways of looking when
sight becomes insight and
the commonplace becomes transfigured
with a new sense of wonder.

This season where everywhere I look I see an explosion of leaves. Deep green, full of life, transforming landscapes. Here the continual miracle of transforming carbon dioxide with the energy of sunshine into sugar and oxygen.

Days of May

In these days of May
there's spring rain, sunshine and
everywhere I look
I see leaves unfurling their secrets.
Deep, fresh and green
Translucent, transparent
thin as gossamer, patterned veined.
Leaves as tangled wildness.
Dancing leaves for healing.
Copper beech leaves in radiant sunshine.
Blizzard of fragrant blossom.
From seed to stem, from tree to leaf
   Another year unfolds to life
      As all creation awakens!

So many of us are on this journey of healing. May we find those coloured kites of hope and hear the blowing of the trumpets in these days.

The Journey of Healing

The Journey of healing is like
crossing high wild mountains, Travelling deeper
into the land layer by layer.
The journey of healing is where
our perspective changes, going higher
than eye can see.
Rising through grey clouds
like coloured kites of hope.
Hearts sound like songbirds singing.
Trumpets blow when healings just begun
when the trail of tears
meets the healing rains
may the healing rains fall again.
Send the rain
the healing rain again.
The healing rain again
Send the rain again.

I wrote this in 2020 in the strange time of lock down. I used to go to the local beach most days, and it seemed like the tide was always out! This matched the feeling of having missed the tide and just being stuck here, but soon I discovered beauty and treasure on that empty beach.

In Sight of The Shore

Came running to the sea again
Only to find that the tide's gone out.
Leaving behind green salt grasses
and cockle pooled shell shore,
        but the tide's gone out.
Light breaks over silver skies,
strong winds blow billowing clouds.
Sands stretched to western seas
        but the tide's gone out.
                Skylarks
dancing between the shades of light,
weaving their patterns across the bay.
Far horizons and white surf turns
        but the tide's gone out.
Beachcombing treasures
In twine tangled webs,
but the tide's gone out.
    And I'm still sat here waiting
        For the turning of the tide.

Summer

….. "As I walk out on this midsummer morning"....

Midsummer. The longest day. No matter what is going on in our individual lives we are reminded that we are part of something bigger that continues to move on, and change is coming!!

Long Days of June

As I walk out on
This midsummer morning.
Trees heavy with green leaves.
High grasses, cow parsley and elder blossom.
Moving out of the cocoon of spring.
There are those of us
who watch and wait
marking days, weeks and seasons
as we approach the full tilt
of earth towards the sun
on this longest day
in this changing world
felt in water, air and sky.
The wheel of the world
still turns again.
Stars weep as war rumbles on
in distant lands.
And we welcome midsummer.

An encounter on a late summer day.

The White Horse

By late August
the bamboo grasses
were taller than me,
and like a cathedral of song
that I walked along, and then
a sudden shaking movement
of a woodland tree, where no winds blew
and no trees moved.
I paused to look and see this thing and
there in the shadows
of these gloomy woods
there you stand looking at me,
serene as you lean against this tree.
A large white horse,
and as our eyes meet
a moment, a movement.
You blink with your sad eyes,
Then we both turn away and with a flick of your
tail
and flash of dazzling dragonfly you've gone
and leave me with this song.
My white horse.

Sleeping out under the stars on the Gower cliffs in Wales as part of a spiritual retreat, then Writing these words after a day of reflective silence at the bottom of the cliffs in the scorching sun...

Three Cliffs Bay

Here I am.
Perched, wedged between the rocks.
Skin and bones squeezed between
these hard places.
Pushed back, confined by incoming tide.
Alone.
Hiding from scorching sun.
And doesn't this describe my life?
Seeking a hiding place from
the unchangeable, unarguable elements.
The absolutes of life.
The sea, rocks and sand
that shaped where I've ended up.
My skin and bones are soft
in comparison to these elements.
There are some things you can't argue
or even dialogue with.
I feel very human this morning.
So aware of vulnerability.

Yes, and now the tide turns.
I see the high mark on the cliffs.
Rocks water-lined.

The tide has turned

and I need to move with this tide.
The tide has turned
and I begin to move out of restriction
and explore again.
I go down to freshly emerging sand
and mark new footprints.
And claim new ground as mine.

As the tide retreats, I continue
this expansion.
Then taking shoes off....
Holy ground
splashing into waters.
Tears rolling down my face.
God, this is intoxicating!
Then two swimmers swim round
from next bay and enter my cove.
My appointment is over.

A visit to Paradise, California in 2019 not long after the terrible fires.

Hell in Paradise - Fires in California

The morning walk and plumes of smoke
are seen upon the ridge.
Then darkness falls
As sun is gone
with choking swirling smoke.
Scorching winds howl through this land
bringing deadly storms of fire
as wall of flames sweep through
destroying all before.
True apocalypse war zone.
Then deathly silence. White ash
Like snow covers burnt out cars
homes and mangled steel.
A town razed raw.
Now walking through these ruins,
we see the painting of his Face.
Beauty in ashes. Tears for Paradise.
And still the birds they sing,
today in Paradise.

My wife and I visited Armenia in the summer of 2019. We loved this ancient nation and even stayed under the shadow of Mount Ararat that was always present. I wrote this at that time.

Ararat of Armenia

There you stand
Hanging in the sky like a precious jewel.
Floating in the clouds.
Ancient Ararat.
Still keeper of secrets in the snow.
Majestic, mysterious mountain of hope
Above the city of winds.
Resplendent with light,
Unveiled suddenly as clouds lift
and sunlight falls.
And sometimes too
there are breathtaking moments
when inner mist lifts
and we glimpse again our Mountain
behind the mountain.
Clear vision, grace rinsed eyes.
Awakened.

It's an early summer morning in Spain and I catch the first sunlight as all nature awakens. I wrote this on a visit in 2018

The Singing Bowl at Alhaurín

First light, and there's orange gardens, ragged
Patchwork of olive groves spread before me.
And behind? The rim of Sierra Nevada.
Encircled by misty blue snow-capped mountains
Creates this singing bowl.
Bark of distant dogs, bullfrogs
In these pastures of heaven.
Fragrance of jasmine, chatter of chaffinch.
As faintest breath of breeze
softly wraps around my skin.

And light pours through these hills.
Multi -layered mountains ripple back
as far as eye can see to sea.
In early morning light flash of swift wing.
At last, this singing bowl
Begins to sing. Awake
dawn chorus just
to bless this
morning.

Autumn

"When autumn leaves fell like dazzling drizzle"

"It's often in the ordinary that we catch a glimpse of the extraordinary and see reality as it really is."

Just a stone on a beach, yet another doorway to walk through. I wrote this in the autumn of 2016 after we spent some time on the beautiful west coast of Scotland, close to the island of Arran.

Stones Of Fire

Today I stumble upon this stone
washed up on Western shores
At low tide in soft evening light.
I watch and see the shimmer
from this ancient rock
as I hold it to the sunset skies.
Feel its warmth on my skin.
Took it home, scrubbed it clean
and see a thin blue vein
in this heart of stone.
Shine it till the light shines through,
till its radiance is glowing.
I'm going to rinse that stone
rub it till the blue shines through,
Glowing like fire.

Sometimes while walking through those glorious pine trees we learn to listen again, breathe and stand tall. I wrote these words after staying for a few weeks in the woods of Oregon in autumn 2017. And it was really like I've written here.

Wisdom Of Trees

And I'm told that
trees breathe through their leaves
as they talk to each other?
Walking through these tall
Stately majestic pine,
Their rich canopy spreading
To the heavens above. Autumn
Leaves falling like golden rain.
Inexhaustible beauty of design.
Flash of blue jay early dawn and
Everywhere the sound of silver singing streams.
Shadows penetrated by light
like some ancient cathedral.
Breathing trees stand serene.
These immense silent firs.
Breathing trees fragrant pine.
Deeply rooted standing tall
Stretching to the heavens,
Teaching me to breathe again
Teaching me to stand
Teaching me to live.
Wisdom of trees

I am always drawn to the sea and have had the good fortune of living close to the sea these last fifteen years. Always a place of encounter.

The Turning of The Tide

I want to go to the sea today
Taste the salt and smell the breeze
Hear the singing of the tides.
Ebb and flow, rise and fall.
Roar begins and falls again.
The swell is deep and deeper still
within. The echo of these seas
The rhythms and riddles of the heart.
Again, the rise and fall.
Again, the ebb and flow.
Again, the growing swell.
Movements of heart.
Knowing I can't hide
from the turning
of the tide.

That moment, those seconds, when everything changes and nothing is the same. August 2018 and we were visiting Ukraine

The Falling

Falling, falling
fierce white light, red heat.
I'm down. Hit the ground.
But not running today.
Piercing, searing knife like
shard of jagged glass,
takes my breath away.
A cry from lips and hip.
That moment when
everything changes....
...and now the ice cold blue steel
and healing scar I carry
tells my story.
Falling, falling
like autumn leaves.
Leaves are falling.

The Journey Home

Early that morning we set out
from the Great Northwest.
Signs in the sky as
wings of wild geese beat high above.
The journey home begins for them as us.
They fly away to safe havens
catching their trade winds.
They're going home. Ah journey home.
I too feel that pull, that prompt
that inner radar, calling me home.
That place of heart belonging.
Place of beginnings
place of roots
place of likeness
mosaic of presence....
...... Then turn oh heart
and walk towards the open door.
Home.

Autumn winds blow cold and birds at the local Wetlands bird sanctuary begin the long journey back to the warmer climates of North Africa and the Mediterranean.

The Great Migration

Across the mountains
of the Great Divide
Like migrating geese
we followed the winds
and crossed the seas.
Like following lost trails
or landlines etched in stone.
Tracing invisible paths
by ancient travellers
finding a rhythm
of new journeys.
Now autumn winds blow cold
scattering gold-streaked leaves.
Now anchored, watching.
Waiting for changing tides
Anchored.
When the light of morning comes
A stairway to silence.
Still anchored.

This journey takes us upwards, always upwards. I wrote this poem in October 2019 when visiting Bangkok, Thailand. I was struck by the new landscapes opening before me. Here there's a new invitation for us to explore. We're hearing different drumbeat others don't hear, glimpsing the new vision, fully alive.

Song Of Ascent

Ascending above this city of trees.
And still the climb. Weary legs.
Above the fluttering sparrows and
Darting swallows.
Above abundant green ferns.
Spreading bamboo and morning glory.
Through early morning mists
Jasmine fragrance drifts.
Sun bleached scorched stone.
Above storms and wilderness
This place of battle silenced.
Now hear the windchimes, far below
the ringing of a distant bell.
At last, I clearly see these far horizons.
Perspective changes, walking with angels.
Now I rest raw, but tender
Within this hidden garden
Where songbirds play
and cool breezes blow,
before moving on again.
Ascending into this fierce light.
Always ascending into the blue.

Winter

" ...Cocooned, weaving our dreams on the loom of our hearts..."

Winter

I've heard it said
That there are days
When diamond dust
Glitters in the still frosty air.
There are days when
we wake up to ice crystals
tumbling out of thick fog.
When glitter floats around
sparkling in bright winter sunshine
like diamonds.
Days when
clouds of diamond dust form
and walking through,
we imprint them with our bodies.
There are days when
Heaven comes close
When eyes are opened
Veils become thin
and glory shines through
in sunburst splendour.
Days when
skins imprinted
with heavens dust
leave us breathless
in His Presence.

Endings and beginnings in this season, as we disappear into winter, and we also reach out to the turning of the year.

Song Of the Turning of the Year

Let winter come
Across these ragged wetlands
Sparkling in the sun.
Now low in the winter sky.
Soft light floods this ancient place
of mists and marshes.
When autumn leaves fell like dazzling drizzle
Blizzard of red rust, gold and copper.
Fragrance of death and decay.
But winter comes between
wind and water, call of the curlew
And the breathing of the trees.
Let winter fall
on the edge of these frontier places.
Still point of the turning world.
Between known and unknown
flows the fire of joy.

Borderlands

We're learning to walk
softly along these borderland trails.
And even lived there for a while.
These ragged places between
the known and the unknown.
The reality and the dream,
Between success and failure,
light and darkness.
Peace and war.
Word and song
Head and heart.
These new frontiers on the edge.
A wide place. No maps here.
To have crossed the Borderlands
and returned with stories to tell?
Ah what stories to tell.
Wild places these Borderlands!
Again they come calling again.

Traveller To the Gate of Wisdom

The sky the day we went away
was clear and blue, now
travelling to this ancient gate
we walk along the path with heart
to the space between the dirt and stars.
Between the edge of sea and shore
The space between two thoughts.
Between the future and the past
The space between two breaths.
We travel on, beyond, to find
the weaver on the loom of life.
The meeting place of heart
I hear it in the deep heart core
cross new thresholds through new doors.
The calling keeps on calling
to find the gift of sound again,
And the gift of sound is
silence.

This poem was written as a collaboration with artist Linda Kelly's painting "Gold, Frankincense and Myrrh, The Art of Suffering" And written in 2020.

Gold, Frankincense and Myrrh

It's out of season you know.
This gold, frankincense and myrrh.
Like so much in our lives at the moment.
And the art of suffering?
I'll stay with the art
and avoid the suffering.
Spent a lifetime doing that
but now radiant gold shines out,
woven into the tapestry of life.
Fragrance of frankincense healing wounds
so costly the scars.
And precious myrrh poured out
transforming pain into beauty.
These tracks of my tears.
These winds that flow into
new rhythms and movements.
These gifts of wisdom to be opened.
Out of the suffering like a river
flows the art soaked with the
fragrance of heaven.

I wrote this in the winter of 2007, not long after we moved to Wales and it's hardly snowed since!

Snowing

It's snowing!
Snowflakes ice flames.
Dazzling crystals of white light
fall softly from frosty skies
bring heavy grace clothing
on hushed earth.
Deep silence.

It's snowing.
All creation falls still
and an unparalleled breathtaking
beauty spreads across the land.
It's snowing!
Sudden blizzard drift,
different perspectives emerge.
New landscapes revealed
bathed in tender light.
Everything's changed.
Innocence restored.
Winter silence.

And so comes the Spirit
to my restless soul.

For Every Season Of Life

"As the stars, so the tides, and so the breath"

Our grandson born in December 2025

First Flight - for Axel

You've travelled far beyond
Your safe harbour. Crossing into open seas.
Leaving behind your soft dreams.
Now beyond tides and turbulence.
Navigating deep waters
Like a young kingfisher you made your home
Nourished, peaceful and undisturbed
Resting in the sanctuary of the riverbed,
you breathed in and filled your lungs.
And now the time to take flight has come
Where an ocean of possibilities awaits.
New worlds to explore.
Now rise and soar as the kingfisher sings
And a new life begins.

Morning Light

And I cradle this
my mug of tea
within my hands today.
Steam rises lazily,
Like me.
Scorching hot blue mug.
Feel the heat burn through
Burning like fire
against my skin.
Now tilt my head back.
Tongue, lips and taste
Feel warmth spread through my body.
Smelling scent of jasmine tea.
Drink deeply now, drink deeply.
Breathe in, breathe out.
I embrace this day
And welcome in the morning.

Your story is unique! Look at your hands. They carry your history. Each life carries its own fingerprints and scars. And nobody on earth really knows our own story except ourselves. I wrote this poem after realising that nobody knew the story of the small scar on my left hand - except me.

Destiny Hands

I've met those who read destiny
by gazing at lines engraved
on the palm of hands,
And me?
I read history in mine.
Look at these hands!
So uniquely fingerprinted.
And who knows their story?
Eight fingers, two thumbs,
two rugged scars.
One gold ring.
Two hands.
One handheld stone that stayed
that night on cliffs when all else
crashed and turned to clay.
One skin.
I'm told that skin holds memories.
In hands now marked by history
we find new creativity.
Come blow new winds of destiny
upon these seeds now blow.

It was 2009. Visiting Sydney, where Captain Cook's first ship arrived, and in a remote Aboriginal community I heard many stories of their history. What pain in the land of tears.

Kamay Botany Bay

Today I'm standing on the edge
of this ragged bay, towards the sea.
The ache, the air, the wind and trees.
And eight days that changed everything.
What was seen by watching eyes?
From where I stand today?
What plague ships came on evening tide
from distant shores to wound the land?
What death winds blew
to scatter life and seed?
An ache, a groan, a sigh, a cry.
And this?
This.
The birthplace of a nation.
Welcome to Australia!

Sanctuary

I return again
And again I return
to that amazing inner sanctuary.
That cathedral of Spirit.
That spacious place
Deep within. Within.

That dwelling of light.
Chamber of heart.
Place of His voice.
Place of His presence.
To this place
I come
Again.

There is a secret pool
of stillness
where gentle breezes ripple
across from distant mountains.
To this place
I return again
Journey
of Heart.

Many cities have lost rivers that still flow underneath them …

Lost Rivers

I've heard it said
That many rivers flow
deep below our greatest cities,
Hidden away, lost, blocked off.
Debris carrying these ghostly rivers.
Still they flow
These lost streams of time.
Now out of sight, out of mind,
covered over built upon.

Now a gentle lapping, distant sigh
and in our own souls too today
lost rivers flow within,
still murmuring.
Lost rivers flow within,
still murmuring.
We still hear it in our deep heart core.
Can you hear the call?
Ghost rivers
still murmuring.

A visit to a bleak hillside in mid Wales where the source of the great rivers Severn and Wye can be found. Always finding the way back to the source.

Springs In the Mountain

Springing up
from the earth.
That clad wet ground
bubbling up, rising.
Sounds of icy water flowing
over singing, dancing stones.
From deep places.
Bubbling up
from the heart of this mountain.

And from this source
wide rivers flow
shaping distant cities.

So now I come to this spring
of streams rising in me.
And wonder
what cities these rivers
of living water will flow to?
What destinies will be shaped?
And how does this rising stream
become a river?

This is the first poem I wrote after a break of 30 years when we moved to South Wales in 2004, joining a very creative community. After a few weeks I wrote these words that I still return to, and I haven't stopped writing since!

Stars, Tides and Breath

Above me, distant constellations
turning, moving.
Beside me waves roll in
turning, crashing on the shore.
Within me the heart beats
I breathe in, breathe out.
Pulse beats to heart rhythm
Pulse beats.

And I?
I know yes!
As the stars, so the tides, and so
the breath.
And so the patterns, colours, rhythms of life.
And so the silence.
The life that I live...
The life that lives in me.

I watch the star patterned sky
Listening to tide turning sea.
Touching the silence.
Part of something bigger,
wider than before.

The Dove in the Stone

Look! Here you come
Sudden flash of white wing
Out of the billowing clouds.
Encircling, enfolded, flutter tongued
This tumbling white dove.
Now resting silent, still.
Your journey from the edge
you come to stone's heart
Welcomed with open hands.
You've found a home in this stone.
This cleft in the rock
Is where you return.
Then spreading your wings
to the soaring winds you go.
And wherever you go
you find your way home
always find your way home
my dove in the stone.

There is such a beauty and mystery to whales. It's fascinating to discover that the communication and songs of whales can travel hundreds, even thousands of miles in deepest oceans. Truly the "record keepers of the history of our planet"

Song Of the Whales

Diving deep, descend to depths,
Then bursting out above the seas
with leaps of joy that dazzle.
These humpbacks, hammerheads.
Blue, white, and orca grey
Whales.
And you know they sing?
Chorusing their
haunting, ancient songs of beauty
echoing across the oceans.
These mountains of the deep.
And sometimes they come to us
in our dreams
to swallow us alive. We sit
incubating deepest darkness
in that whale belly.
Till hurled out again
staggering onto dry land
we're restored to life,
Stepping forward through
the Gates of Awakening
embracing new destiny
fully awake now
Yes, fully alive again.

Always that call comes again to go deeper.

Deeper

Plunging into deeper waters,
Out of my depth again.
Water droplets dance like crystal
alive with sunlight
over my head.
Breathless

And now my heart is still,
wrapped in silence.
Wholly attentive,
returning to its root,
that point of turning.
No turning back.
Still.

Sitting in darkness and the miracle of transformation happens again. Sometimes it seems unlikely, often unrecognised or ignored but I'm so glad that it comes afresh to our troubled world. Light floods in and it's a new day. I wrote this poem in 2017 after staying in Spain where I would often be up early on the flat roof and in the darkness watch for the dawn.

Toward the Dawn - Sierra Nevada

I remember
those moments in darkness
silently sitting waiting for sunrise
And the returning light of dawn
across the snowy mountain range.
I wonder, but will it really come today?
Then slowly, so slowly
over the horizon I see
a golden glow of fire.
Shadows shrink, light pours in
and shimmers across the skies,
Land soaked with gold.
Stained with light.
Again, I honour the miracle
of transformation.
Sunrise.

And the river flows on, and so the dance continues.

Trinity Song

And that river of glory
that flows cascading full of
passion, presence, beauty, joy.
That twisting, dancing river
through and out beyond me flows.
That song rising.
That great dance, rhythm of life
flowing, swirling, flowing life.

My Father, Son and Spirit.
Circling love enfolded
through and out beyond me flows.
Circling life extending.

And you came again to me
lifting, weaving fragments, parts
streams of life.
Joining me to your laughing
great joyful triumphant dance.
Three in one
    I worship
        You.

Seven Years - for Issie

We've seen the Blue Mountains of Australia
Sailed on that old pearling ship in Darwin harbour
With a breath-taking sunset.
Seen bushfires along the Katherine Gorge
highway
where we sat with the aboriginal women.
Rode the night train along the Pacific,
travelled to stay amongst those beautiful woods
of Oregon, and oh those glorious colours of
autumn.
We walked along that walled city of Chiang Mai
And dreamed at the ancient gates.
The markets and music of Chiang Rai too.
Rode the night train across the Ukraine.
We stood under the stars of the stunning Southern
Cross.
Saw thermal springs and swam under the stars.
Saw blackened, burnt-out Paradise after the fires.
And Spain became a second home for a season.
Like migrating swallows, we followed the winds.
Now anchored, Watching for changing tides
Still anchored

The most important journey is our journey home....
Written after a visit to Ireland in 2019.

The Lighthouse

There's a fragment of dream here,
or memory perhaps
of the roar of wild seas
crashing shingled seashore.
Breathing in, breathing out.
And there you are soaring above
the old white lighthouse,
still shining out
through this winter storm.
There's a light in the window
that's calling me home
Still point of a turning world.
Returning again
to where I belong.
This my house of light.
This my house of stone.
This my place called home.
Always on my journey.
Home.

Acknowledgements

Many thanks to my wife Issie for all her editing, and our family Phil and Sarah, Michelle and Rory and our grandchildren Bella, Finlay and now young Axel for their encouragement and love in listening, reading and standing with me in this book project.

For my brother Andrew, who gave me a couple of poetry books as a teenager that I still read, and which inspired me to read Dylan Thomas, and for my sister Pauline for her continuous encouragement.

Thanks to El for all your enormous practical help in the last part of publishing this book.

Also special thanks to Karen Lowe who reawakened the flame for writing poetry after many years of neglect.

www.ingramcontent.com/pod-product-compliance
Lightning Source LLC
La Vergne TN
LVHW051020080826
845145LV00009B/2722